Preston Public Library

Preston, CT 06365

PRESTON PUBLIC LIBRARY

J
974.5
JOS

Joseph, Paul
        Rhode Island /

The United States

Rhode Island

Paul Joseph
ABDO & Daughters

visit us at
www.abdopub.com

Published by Abdo & Daughters, 4940 Viking Drive, Suite 622, Edina, Minnesota 55435.
Copyright © 1998 by Abdo Consulting Group, Inc., Pentagon Tower, P.O. Box 36036,
Minneapolis, Minnesota 55435 USA. International copyrights reserved in all countries.
No part of this book may be reproduced in any form without written permission from the
publisher.

Printed in the United States.

Cover and Interior Photo credits: Peter Arnold, Inc., SuperStock, Archive

Edited by Lori Kinstad Pupeza
Contributing editor Brooke Henderson
Special thanks to our Checkerboard Kids—Priscilla Cáceres, Teddy Borth, Jack Ward,
Aisha Baker

All statistics taken from the 1990 census; The Rand McNally Discovery Atlas of The
United States.

Library of Congress Cataloging-in-Publication Data

Joseph, Paul, 1970-
    Rhode Island / Paul Joseph.
    p. cm. -- (The United States)
    Includes index.
    Summary: Surveys the people, geography, and history of the northeastern state
    nicknamed "Little Rhody."
    ISBN 1-56239-877-6
    1. Rhode Island--Juvenile literature. [1. Rhode Island.] I. Title. II. Series:
    United States (Series)
    F79.3.J67   1998
    974.5--dc21
                                                        97-21417
                                                        CIP
                                                        AC

Contents

Welcome to Rhode Island

Rhode Island is known for being the smallest state in the Union. However, with just over a million people, only seven other states have less **population**.

Even though the state is very small, it is rich in history, tradition, people, and beauty. Throughout United States history, Rhode Island has been a very important state. It was even one of the original 13 colonies.

The state was first called the State of Rhode Island and Providence Plantations. Later, it was shortened to simply Rhode Island.

Some historians think the name came from the Dutch words *roodt eylandt*. This is translated in English to "red island." When sailors first saw the island they noticed the red shoreline from the red clay and rocks.

Others say the name came from the Greek Island, Rhodes. Some people today call the state "Little Rhody." This is a popular nickname reflecting its size.

The Rhode Island coastline

Fast Facts

RHODE ISLAND

Capital and Largest city
Providence (160,728 people)
Area
1,054 square miles
(2,730 sq km)
Population
1,005,984 people
Rank: 43rd
Statehood
May 29, 1790
(13th state admitted)
Principal rivers
Blackstone River, Providence
River
Highest point
Jerimoth Hill;
812 feet (247 m)
Motto
Hope
Song
"Rhode Island"
Famous People
Ambrose Burnside, George M.
Cohan, Nathanael Greene,
Matthew C. and Oliver Perry,
Gilbert Stuart

Rhode Island is one of the original 13 colonies

*S*tate Flag

*V*iolet

*R*hode Island Red

*R*ed Maple

About Rhode Island

The Ocean State

Detail area

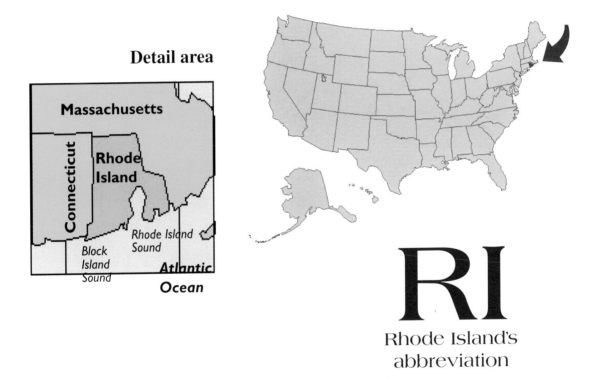

RI

Rhode Island's
abbreviation

Borders: west (Connecticut), north (Massachusetts),
east (Massachusetts), south (Atlantic Ocean)

Nature's Treasures

The beautiful state of Rhode Island has many treasures in its state. For a small state it has many different types of natural treasures. There are forests, lakes, rivers, highlands, lowlands, sandy beaches, salt marshes, and the **Atlantic Ocean.**

Water is by far Rhode Island's best treasure. People use the water of the lakes, rivers, streams, and ocean for many different activities.

Some people use Rhode Island's water for fun like boating, swimming, fishing, and water-skiing. Other water activities are used for work. **Fisheries** sell the fish they catch. Some of the fish caught are clam, lobster, squid, sea mussel, butterfish, mackerel, and cod. And huge boats bring many different things to sell in and out of the state.

Rhode Island's land also is a treasure. Potatoes, hay, corn, apples, and peaches are some of the leading **crops**. The land of Rhode Island is excellent for animals to **graze**.

Underground, stone, sand, and gravel can be found. These are the most valuable **minerals** found in the state.

Narragansett Bay off the coast of Rhode Island

Beginnings

The first known people to settle in Rhode Island were **Native Americans**. Some of these Native Americans that were living there were the Narraganset, Niantic, Nipmuc, Pequot, and Wampanoag.

In 1614, Dutch captain Adriaen Block sailed along the coast of Rhode Island. The island right off the mainland is named for him. Block Island is also a city.

The actual founder of Rhode Island was Roger Williams. He came to Rhode Island in 1636. He started the first settlement and named the town Providence. Soon after, many people came to Rhode Island looking for religious freedom.

In 1639, John Clark and William Coddington **founded** the town of Newport. In the same year the first Baptist church in America was formed in Providence.

Rhode Island was the first American state to declare its independence from England in 1776. Although Rhode Island was one of the original 13 colonies, it was the last to agree to the Constitution. Finally on May 29, 1790, Rhode Island **ratified** the Constitution and became the 13th state.

The signing of the Declaration of Independence.

B.C. to 1639

Early People, Land, and Cities
During the Ice Age, many thousands of years ago, Rhode Island was covered by ice and glaciers. Many years later the ice began to melt and the land of Rhode Island began to form.

The first known people living in Rhode Island were **Native Americans**. They were the Narraganset, Niantic, Nipmuc, Pequot, and Wampanoag.

1636: Roger Williams **founds** the city of Providence.

1638: John Clark and William Coddington found the city of Pocasset (now Portsmouth). In 1639, Clark and Coddington found Newport.

Rhode Island

B.C. to 1639

1664 to 1700s

Establishing Statehood

1664: Block Island is made a part of Rhode Island.

1727: The first printing press in Rhode Island is set up in Newport.

1764: Rhode Island College is **founded** at Warren. In 1770, it was moved to Providence. In 1804, it was renamed Brown University.

1776: Rhode Island is the first colony to declare independence over England.

1790: Rhode Island becomes the 13th state on May 29.

Rhode Island

1664 to 1700s

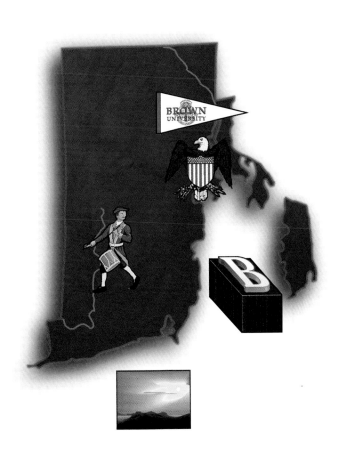

1800s to Now

Industry, Bridges, and Colleges

1818: Jabez Gorham starts the state's silverware **industry** in Providence.

1888: University of Rhode Island is **founded** at Kingston.

1969: The Newport Bridge between Newport and Jamestown is completed.

1987: Providence College makes it to the Final Four in men's college basketball.

Rhode Island

1800s to Now

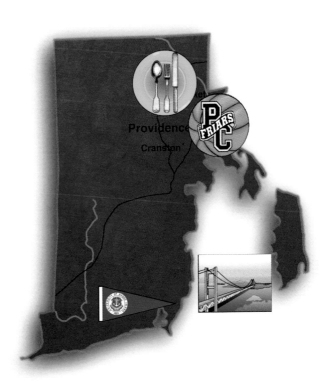

Providence

Cranston

Rhode Island's People

There are just over one million people in the state of Rhode Island. It is the 43rd least **populated** state in country. The first known group to live in the state were **Native Americans**.

Today, many well-known people have made Rhode Island home. One of the greatest baseball players of all time was born and raised in Woonsocket, Rhode Island. Nap Lajoie started playing in the major leagues in 1896, for the Philadelphia Phillies. In 1902, he joined the Cleveland Broncos who later changed their name to the Naps in honor of Lajoie. When playing for the Athletics, his batting average in 1901 was .422. It's the highest in American League history.

Other famous people from Rhode Island include James Burrill Angell who was a professor, diplomat, and journalist. Movie-star Nelson Eddy was born in Providence.

President John F. Kennedy made Rhode Island his summer home. The Hammersmith Mansion in Newport, Rhode Island, was called the summer White House because Kennedy spent most of the summers there when he was president. Today, his nephew, Patrick Kennedy, is a United States Representative from Rhode Island. Patrick is the son of the United States Senator of Massachusetts, Edward (Teddy) Kennedy.

Nelson Eddy

Patrick Kennedy

Splendid Cities

Rhode Island has many splendid cities in the state with a lot of things to offer. About 75 percent of Rhode Island's people live within 15 miles (24 km) of the city of Providence. However, outside of that area are many other wonderful cities.

Providence is located on the Providence River at the head of the Narragansett Bay. It is known for its jewelry and silver making. Providence is a very well-known city throughout the nation. It is filled with history, many fine colleges, and a lot of **tourist** attractions.

Providence is not only the capital of Rhode Island but also the largest city, with about 160,000 people.

Newport is a **resort** town known for its incredible resorts and fabulous mansions right on the water. It is also the scene of yacht races and famous jazz festivals. The International Tennis Hall of Fame and Tennis Museum is located in Newport.

Warwick is the second largest city with about 85,000 people. It is a very nice city that is near Providence. Other splendid cities include, Cranston, Pawtucket, Coventry, and Woonsocket.

Newport Harbor and Bay Bridge in Newport, RI.

Rhode Island's Land

During the Ice Age, many thousands of years ago, Rhode Island was covered by huge glaciers. After these great ice sheets began to melt, the land of Rhode Island began to form. The land is divided into two areas, the New England Upland and the Seaboard Lowland.

The New England Upland region is in the western half of the state. It reaches into Connecticut and Massachusetts. The area is a rough and hilly plateau. It is filled with many lakes and forests. Rhode Island's highest point is in this region. It is Jerimoth Hill, which is 812 feet (247 m) tall.

New England Upland

Seaboard Lowland

Narragansett Bay

The Seaboard Lowland is in the eastern half of the state. This shallow lowland area extends into southeastern Massachusetts. It is also part of the Appalachian Highlands. There are many sandy beaches and salt marshes in this area.

The Seaboard Lowland is known for its rivers. These include the Providence, Pawtuxet, and Blackstone rivers that all flow to Narragansett Bay. The Pawcatuck River drains into Worden Pond.

The Rhode Island shoreline in winter.

Rhode Island at Play

The people of Rhode Island and the many people who visit the state have a lot of things to do. For more than 200 years, vacationers have made the seashores of Rhode Island their favorite place to visit.

Newport is one of the oldest **resorts** in the United States. People began visiting as early as the middle 1800s. There are many ocean side mansions that have been turned into museums.

Other popular resorts in Rhode Island include Watch Hill, Block Island, and Narragansett. Some of the fun things to do at these resorts are swim, sunbathe, boat, and fish.

Narragansett Bay has been the site of the International America's Cup boat races and the Classic Yacht Regatta.

Other places of interest in Rhode Island include museums, colleges, state parks, monuments, lakes, forests, and rivers. It is no wonder people have played in Rhode Island for more than 200 years. Even President John F. Kennedy and his family made it their favorite vacation spot.

The Rhode Island coastline is a popular vacation spot.

Rhode Island at Work

The people of Rhode Island must work to make money. Many work in or around large cities, while others work in **rural** communities. Most of the people in the state work in service.

Even though Rhode Island is small, it is still one of the most highly **industrialized** states in the country. About 33 percent of Rhode Island's workers are employed in **manufacturing**.

Nehemiah Dodge, a goldsmith and watch repairer began manufacturing jewelry in Rhode Island in the 1790s. Today, Rhode Island is the country's leading costume jewelry center in the United States.

Other things made in Rhode Island are metals, electrical equipment, and ships.

Some people in Rhode Island are farmers. Potatoes, hay, corn, apples, and peaches are among the leading **crops** grown. Other people work in **fisheries**. People work in many different jobs.

Rhode Island offers many different things to do and see. Because of its natural beauty, people, land, coast, and **resorts**, Little Rhody is a great place to visit, live, work, and play.

Boats and ships are made in Rhode Island.

Fun Facts

•For over 100 years Rhode Island had two state capitals. They were Newport and Providence. **Legislature** would meet every other time in each city. Finally, in 1900, the state capital was moved to only Providence where it still is today.

•Rhode Island's state boundaries were not decided for many years. Rhode Island became a state in 1790 but the western boundary with Connecticut was not settled until 1887. The northern boundary with Massachusetts was settled in 1883 and the eastern boundary was finally settled in 1899.

•Rhode Island is the smallest state in the country. However, in **population**, seven other states are smaller.

•Rhode Island is actually 36 small islands and one big mainland.

•The greatest length of Rhode Island from north to south is only 59 miles (95 km). The state's greatest width from east to west is only 40 miles (64 km). It would take a person less than one hour to drive from the very bottom of the state to the very top. It is no wonder the state is nicknamed Little Rhody!

The Rhode Island State House in Providence.

Glossary

Atlantic Ocean: one of a few large seas that surround continents. This one borders the entire East Coast of the United States, including the southern coast of Rhode Island.

Border: neighboring states, countries, or waters.

Crops: what farmers grow on their farm to eat and sell.

Fisheries: the business of catching fish.

Found: to take the first steps in building or starting something.

Graze: animals eating grass.

Industrial: big businesses such as factories or manufacturing.

Industry: a kind of business. Those who work in the computer industry make, sell, or fix computers.

Legislature: a group of people elected by the citizens of the state to represent them and make laws.

Manufacture: to make things by machine in a factory.

Minerals: things found in the earth, such as rock, diamonds, or coal.

Native Americans: the first people who were born in and occupied North America.

Population: the number of people living in a certain place.

Ratified: to agree upon something and approve it formally.

Resort: a place to vacation that has fun things to do.

Rural: outside of a big city, or in the country.

Tourists: people who travel for pleasure.

Internet Sites

Narragansett Bay, Rhode Island
http://inlet.geol.sc.edu/NAR/home.html
This site gives you general information, site descriptions, research projects, educational projects, and more. As far as the Island's environment, it is a very informative site.

This site is subject to change. Go to your favorite search engine and type in Rhode Island for more sites.

PASS IT ON

Tell Others Something Special About Your State
To educate readers around the country, pass on interesting tips, places to see, history, and little known facts about the state you live in. We want to hear from you!
To get posted on ABDO & Daughters website, e-mail us at "mystate@abdopub.com"

Index